GW00391829

# KING ROLLO
## and the tree
## David McKee

*Andersen Press · London*

*Hutchinson Australia*

© 1980 David McKee.  ISBN 0 905478 70 3

**King Rollo was in the garden.**

"I'm going to climb that tree," he said.

"Don't climb the tree, you'll get your hands dirty," said the magician.

"I'm still going to climb that tree,"
said King Rollo.

"Don't climb the tree, you will tear your jacket," said Cook.

"I'm going to climb very high," said
King Rollo.

"Don't climb the tree, you'll fall and hurt yourself," said Queen Gwen.

"I'm going to climb right to the top,"
said King Rollo.

Hamlet the cat said nothing.

King Rollo started to climb.

"Mmm," said the magician.

King Rollo climbed and climbed.

"Tut, tut," said Cook.

King Rollo climbed very high.

"Oh dear," said Queen Gwen.

King Rollo climbed right to the very
top.

Then King Rollo slipped.

All the way down the tree he slipped
and slid and slid and slipped.

**Finally he landed on the ground with a BUMP!**

"I said you would get your hands
dirty," said the magician.

"I said you would tear your jacket,"
said Cook.

"I said you would fall and hurt yourself," said Queen Gwen.

"And I said I would climb to the top,"
said King Rollo.

"Yes," said Queen Gwen, "and you did."

Printed in Great Britain by W. S. Cowell Ltd., Ipswich